THE DANGER OF "UN-PASTORED" PASTORS

Bishop Adrian R. Rodgers & Bishop Ron Webb

REJOICE
Essential Publishing

Bishop Adrian R. Rodgers & Bishop Ron Webb/Rejoice Essential Publishing

PO BOX 512

Effingham, SC 29541

www.republishing.org

Unless otherwise indicated, scripture is taken from the King James Version.'

Scripture quotations marked MSG are taken from The Message, copyright © 1993, 2002, 2018 by Eugene H. Peterson. Used by permission of NavPress. All rights reserved. Represented by Tyndale House Publishers.

The Danger of "Un-Pastored" Pastors/Bishop Adrian R. Rodgers & Bishop Ron Webb

ISBN-13: 978-1-956775-91-4

TABLE OF CONTENTS

FOREWORD

I am honored to have been invited to write a foreword for your first book. You have talked about this book being published for quite some time, and our good, good Father has helped you and your co-author bring it to fruition.

Your spiritual journey under the guidance of your natural father, Bishop Charles Rodgers, has been truly remarkable. His teachings have instilled in you a deep sense of service, which you have exemplified in your relationship with him. Witnessing your continued honor for him and your eagerness to seek his counsel is heartening.

This book is a treasure trove of profound wisdom and spiritual insights. I am confident that its readers will be enriched and blessed by its contents.

My prayer is that God will help those who have been unwilling or have had reservations about being fathered realize that every man and woman that have been assigned to ministry in any capacity needs to be fathered.

I am proud of you and honor you as my husband, my natural covering, and as my Pastor, my spiritual covering. I pray that God will continue to bless you as you have been a spiritual father to many and as you continue to be a spiritual father to many more.

With love and honor from your wife,

Constance D. DeBerry-Rodgers

INTRODUCTION

"God said, Let us make man in our image, after our likeness: and let them have dominion over the fish of the sea, and over the fowl of the air, and over the cattle, and over all the earth, and over every creeping thing that creepeth upon the earth. 27 So God created man in his own image, in the image of God created he him; male and female created he them" (Genesis 1:26-27 KJV). God created man for His own purpose and when He did, He had a will and purpose for his life.

"For I know the thoughts that I think toward you, saith the LORD, thoughts of peace, and not of evil, to give you an expected end" (Jerimiah 29:11 KJV). God created man to protect, provide and lead the house for which they cover. However, the world has begun to radically change the family structure God originally created. With the social, economic, and technical advances of the 20th century came a basic change in the structure and function of the family — with a consequent shift in the authority of the father. His influence is now increasingly seen as minor, even negligible, and his importance has now decreased in value (Ditta M. Oliker, 2011). And because the value of a father has decreased within households, the value of being fathered has decreased within the church. Many Christians who attend church are not used to submitting to a male figure because they lacked a father figure in their household.

In a time when the percentage of absent fathers in households continues to increase, leaders in the Christian faith lack the desire to seek spiritual guidance from male authority. One may suggest the lack of fathers in the physical house parallels the lack of fathers in the church house. Therefore, many Christian leaders are failing to heed instruction and the proper guidance to conduct ministry, which then leads to the suffering of the Christian Faith. Hence, to provide a solution and to understand the root cause of this ongoing issue, this book will explore the purpose of family created by God, the destruction of families, the dangers of absent fathers, and the correlation between the lack of fathers in the house and church house, and how to transition from the un-fathered to the fathered.

CHAPTER I

GOD'S PURPOSE FOR FAMILY AND FATHERS

BISHOP ADRIAN RODGERS' PERSPECTIVE

The family is important, necessary, and foundational because God created it to be so (Gritters, 1998). Family was the first institution God created for His glory. God first made Adam and from Adam, Eve was made. When God made Adam, He created him from dust, whereas, when He created Eve, He did that out of Adam. Therefore, Eve was not independent, but was made a helper, and perfectly "fit" for Adam; this is the idea of the word "help-meet" according to *Genesis 2:18* in the King James Version (Aust, 2014).

A part of family is marriage and God instructed the man to leave his father and mother and cleave to his wife, making him the head of his household. A man leaving his parents does not mean he is abandoning his parents, but he must see that his wife and family created with his wife is most important. Cleaving means "clinging to, holding dearly." This refers to a covenant commitment by the husband and wife to each other. They are, as it were, bonded together. When two become one, man and wife, they become one flesh, "Wherefore they are no more twain, but one flesh." This refers to the sexual union, but we should not limit it to that. Husbands and wives become one in their entire nature--their thinking, hopes, sorrows, and joys" (Matthew 19:6).

Since marriage is a creation of God, we must obey God's regulations for marriage:

- one man for one woman
- sex only for marriage
- no divorce, except for fornication or adultery
- the man is the head of the woman.
- husbands love your wives.
- wives submit to your husbands.

Daughters and sons grow up to get married. The example the father sets is generally the one adult children emulate.

The men of families were created to be fathers. The father is to provide for his family, which was established from the beginning of time. The Bible says in *Genesis 2:15 (The Message Bible) God took the Man and set him down in the Garden of Eden to work the ground and keep it in order.* It is the order of God for the man to work so he can provide for his family.

The Bible also says in *1 Timothy 5:8 (The King James Version), "But if any provide not for his own, and specially for those of his own house, he hath denied the faith, and is worse than an infidel."* A father who loves the Lord will do everything within his power to provide for his family. In this age of common law marriage or "shacking" as it is called by many, there are women who are working while the man is home playing video games or running the streets in her car! Some will even pick the woman they live with up from work late simply because he had another woman in her car. This is the kind of foolishness that happens when things are not carried out in God's way. A real father provides not only for now, but he also plans for the future; understanding that children are going to grow up, graduate, become viable members of society, and join the working class. Another role for a father is to protect and set boundaries for the family.

"God commanded the Man, You can eat from any tree in the garden, [17] except from the Tree-of-Knowledge-of-Good-and-Evil. Don't eat from it. The moment you eat from that tree, you're dead." — *Genesis 2:16-17 (The Message Bible)*

Unfortunately, Adam did not protect and set boundaries for his family in this instance. Therefore, it changed the course of the world. God gave the command to the man. The woman should not have been talking to the devil; however, Adam should have stepped up and handled the situation. The father or husband should be willing to make even unpopular decisions to protect and set boundaries for his family. It is important for fathers to realize, as it relates to their children, that it is their responsibility to be the head of the house and not the friend. Many times, the decisions a father must make will not be liked, particularly when the children are in their teenage years. The teenage years are difficult when challenges from the child to adult ratio increases to most often. While some mothers are prone to make emotional decisions to keep the mother/child friend status, a father must make solid, firm decisions and stand on them. A father must also be a leader who provides the direction and guidance for the entire family.

"If you decide that it's a bad thing to worship God, then choose a god you'd rather serve, and do it today. Choose one of the gods your ancestors worshiped from the country beyond The River, or one of the gods of the Amorites, on whose land you're now living. As for me

and my family, we'll worship God." — Joshua 24:15 (The Message Bible).

Joshua spoke for his family when he said, "As for me and my family, we'll worship God." Every family needs clear leadership! It is important to understand that deep down, the wife and children want to be led. The godly wife wants to be led by her husband. Children want to be led by their father. Remember, children repeat the behavior they experienced. This is not always the case, but it is most often the case.

"He must handle his own affairs well, attentive to his own children and having their respect." — (The Message Bible)

Fathers should also serve the household as the spiritual head. It is so critical the father is biblically saved in addition to being the spiritual head in the home. Life is so much easier when both Father and Mother love the Lord. They should live a holy life in front of the children and lead them to church. According to statistics, when a mother comes to Christ, her family will join her at church only 17% of the time, but when a father comes to Christ, his family joins him 93% of the time (Why Men Matter- Both Now and Forever). These statistics confirm the spiritual and biological difference that fathers make in the household.

When a father and mother live in a manner which exemplifies a healthy marriage relationship, it teaches daughters what to expect and sons learn what they should do. Healthy households are more likely to prevent children from having unrealistic expectations as aforementioned.

1 Peter 3:7 a,b (KJV) - Likewise, ye husbands, dwell with them according to knowledge, giving honour unto the wife, as unto the weaker vessel,

The spiritually and emotionally healthy father will honor the woman as physically weaker. He should not expect her to do the heavy lifting physically or emotionally. The father should recognize his wife as a joint heir of the grace of God, according to scripture. Not recognizing this biblical principle will cause his prayers to be hindered according to 1 Peter 3:7c.

1 Peter 3:7c (KJV) - ... and as being heirs together of the grace of life; that your prayers be not hindered.

CHAPTER II

GOD'S PURPOSE FOR SPIRITUAL FATHERS

BISHOP ADRIAN RODGERS' PERSPECTIVE

Elijah and Elisha

The beginning of this relationship started in *1 Kings 19:19-21 (The King James Version), which says that* [19] *So he departed thence, and found Elisha the son of Shaphat, who was plowing with twelve yoke of oxen before him, and he with the twelfth: and Elijah passed by him, and cast his mantle upon him.* [20] *And he left the oxen, and ran after Elijah, and said, Let me, I pray thee, kiss my father and my mother, and then I will follow thee. And he said unto him, Go back again: for what have I done to thee?* [21] *And he returned back from him, and took a yoke of oxen, and slew them, and boiled their flesh with the instruments of the oxen, and gave unto the people, and they did eat. Then he arose, and went after Elijah, and ministered unto him.*

This passage of scripture shows that even though Elisha did not know who Elijah was, Elisha immediately trusted the man of God. His trust was based on the relationship that he had with God for himself.

Because three verses earlier God spoke to Elijah and instructed him to anoint Elisha as his replacement. From this time forward, Elisha served Elijah and learned from him as his disciple. In this story, Elijah stood for the spiritual father and mentor, while Elisha was the spiritual son.

The Bible says in *2 Kings 2:1-6 (KJV)* *"And it came to pass, when the LORD would take up Elijah into heaven by a whirlwind, that Elijah went with Elisha from Gilgal. ² And Elijah said unto Elisha, Tarry here, I pray thee; for the LORD hath sent me to Bethel. And Elisha said unto him, As the LORD liveth, and as thy soul liveth, I will not leave thee. ³ And the sons of the prophets that were at Bethel came forth to Elisha, and said unto him, Knowest thou that the LORD will take away thy master from thy head to day? And he said, Yea, I know it; hold ye your peace. ⁴ And Elijah said unto him, Elisha, tarry here, I pray thee; for the LORD hath sent me to Jericho. And he said, As the LORD liveth, and as thy soul liveth, I will not leave thee. So they came to Jericho. ⁵ And the sons of the prophets that were at Jericho came to Elisha, and said unto him, Knowest thou that the LORD will take away thy master from thy head to day? And he answered, Yea, I know it; hold ye your peace. ⁶ And Elijah said unto him, Tarry, I pray thee, here; for the LORD hath sent me to Jordan. And he said, As the LORD liveth, and as thy soul liveth, I will not leave thee. And they two went on."*

We do not know just how long Elijah's servant had been with him before he became his successor. But clearly, Elisha had formed a strong bond with his master. Within 2 Kings 2:7–18, Authur Lee Woofenden notes that three times Elijah told Elisha to stay behind while Elijah traveled to another place. Instead, Elisha refused and instead stuck by his master's side (Woofenden, 2020). In exploring this passage of scripture, one can understand that Elijah committed his life to serve Elisha. In this context Elisha is a spiritual father preparing to pass the mantle to his spiritual son. This text is especially important because it shows total commitment to the leader without hesitation. Not only was Elisha the spiritual son in this story, but he also served as Elijah's assistant. Elisha was not an easy man to serve. This is shown even at the onset of the relationship as Elijah did not wait for Elisha. This teaches us that when God has assigned a mentor and spiritual father, the son does not dictate the demeanor.

"⁷ And fifty men of the sons of the prophets went, and stood to view afar off: and they two stood by Jordan. ⁸ And Elijah took his mantle, and wrapped it together, and smote the waters, and they were divided hither and thither, so that they two went over on dry ground. ⁹ And it came to pass, when they were gone over, that Elijah said unto Elisha, Ask what I shall do for thee, before I be taken away from thee. And Elisha said, I pray thee, let a double portion of thy spirit be upon me. ¹⁰ And he said, Thou hast asked a hard thing: nevertheless, if thou see me when I am taken from thee, it shall be so unto thee; but if not, it shall not be so. ¹¹ And it came to pass, as they still went on, and talked, that, behold, there appeared a chariot of fire, and horses of fire, and parted them both asunder; and Elijah went up by a whirlwind into heaven. ¹² And Elisha saw it, and he cried, My father, my father, the chariot of Israel, and the horsemen thereof. And he saw him no more: and he took hold of his own clothes, and rent them in two pieces. ¹³ He took up also the mantle of Elijah that fell from him, and went back, and stood by the bank of Jordan" (2 Kings 2:7-13 The King James Version).

Instead of feeling entitled and feeling like he was owed this mantle and promotion, Authur Lee Woofenden states Elijah's approach was quite different. Elisha became a servant to Elijah. Instead of being cared for, he had to take care of his master's needs which included pouring his water, and washing his feet. As a servant, Elisha had to endure the same hardships Elijah did. Before Elijah could make the decision to pass on his mantle, he had to know that Elisha had enough iron ribbing in his character to withstand the harsh challenges of being a prophet of the Lord in a hostile world. To the very end, Elijah tested Elisha to see if he could be too easily turned away from the hard road he must travel (Woofenden, 2020). You see, sometimes serving is not pleasant and it certainly is not glamorous. I have known some people who served as armor bearers who only served to try to be noticed by others. For that reason, they were always in the way and were more interested in being noticed than serving.

Bystanders seemed to be looking for God to immediately put His stamp of approval on Elisha by allowing his first miracle to be Elijah's last miracle. As soon as this miracle was performed by Elisha, the people knew that Elisha's new place was God's idea and with God's approval.

"And he took the mantle of Elijah that fell from him, and smote the waters, and said, "Where is the LORD God of Elijah? and when he also had smitten the waters, they parted hither and thither: and Elisha went over. [15] And when the sons of the prophets which were to view at Jericho saw him, they said, The spirit of Elijah doth rest on Elisha. And they came to meet him, and bowed themselves to the ground before him." (2 Kings 2:14-15 The King James Version). When you have honored, respected, and served others, you will be honored, respected, and served.

CHAPTER III

THE INTERVIEW

BISHOP RON WEBB'S PERSPECTIVE

1 Corinthians 4:15 says, "For though ye have ten thousand in-structers in Christ, yet have ye not many fathers: for in Christ Jesus I have begotten you through the gospel."

During my interviews with pastors, bishops, overseers, and leaders, I was deeply moved by their personal experiences and the wisdom they shared. As they have proven to be faithful followers, I found their insights to be spiritual nuggets that I will forever cherish.

I want to focus on two main topics in this chapter. The first is the blessing of a spiritual father and the benefits of having that spiritual covering.

1. Protection-covering-blessing-favor-support.
2. A spiritual father helps push you into your destiny.
3. They help point you toward purpose.
4. They cultivate an environment of identity.
5. They empower you by developing powerful relationships.
6. True spiritual fathers desire for those around them to excel beyond their reach and surpass their level of growth.

7. Their agenda is never about control or limiting but rather pouring confidence in them.
8. They tell you when you're doing it the right way.
9. They tell you when you're doing it the wrong way.
10. They rebuke you in love.
11. He's your connection to your future.
12. They give direction and correction at the same time.
13. They tell you when to speak up and tell you when to shut it up.

Every true man and woman of God stands in a place of success and victory because someone prayed for them, prayed with them, and prayed over them. This transformative power of prayer and spiritual guidance is a testament to the importance of having a spiritual father.

1. Some confessed that their destiny was delayed because they didn't have a spiritual father or overseer.
2. They felt at times unprotected, disconnected, and lonely
3. No accountability.
4. No spiritual well to draw from.
5. No spiritual counselor.
6. Many mistakes of not having a mentor.

So here are just a few comments of a blessing of a spiritual covering and a cursing without one.

CHALLENGES OF NOT HAVING A SPIRITUAL LEADER

1. **Lack of spiritual guidance:** Without a spiritual father, individuals may struggle to find someone to provide spiritual guidance, support, and advice in times of need.
2. **Challenges in understanding and interpreting religious texts:** A spiritual father is often trained in theology and bibli-

cal interpretation, making it easier for individuals to understand and interpret religious texts on their own.

3. **Difficulty building a sense of community:** Spiritual fathers play a key role in building and maintaining a sense of community within a religious setting. Without a spiritual father, individuals may find it challenging to connect with others on a spiritual level.

4. **Lack of pastoral care:** Spiritual fathers often provide pastoral care to individuals going through difficult times, such as illness, grief, or relationship issues. Without a spiritual father, individuals may lack the necessary support and comfort during these challenging times.

5. Always feeling disconnected.

6. Experiencing severe loneliness.

7. There would have been less mistakes made.

BLESSING OF HAVING A SPIRITUAL LEADER

1. **Spiritual guidance:** A spiritual father can provide guidance, support, and the blessings of spiritual counseling based on their knowledge of religious beliefs and practices. It's a blessing to have wisdom or sound advice from your spiritual father. My spiritual father taught me how to train the church to be a spirit led church instead of a deacon controlled church.

2. **Community support:** Spiritual fathers often play a central role in the community, providing support, organizing community events, and serving as a source of comfort and assistance in times of need. My spiritual father gave me the blessings of his endorsements.

3. **Leadership:** The spiritual father provides leadership within the church, helping to guide and support the congregation in their spiritual journey. It's a blessing to be able to call and ask questions about making major decisions. It's a blessing

to have your spiritual father's presence at board meetings. He taught me how to handle accusations or even if I should respond at all.

4. **Teaching and preaching:** Spiritual fathers deliver sermons, teach classes, and lead worship services, helping to educate and inspire their congregation.

5. **Sacraments:** The spiritual father administers sacraments such as baptism, communion, and marriage, providing important spiritual milestones for the congregation.

6. **Crisis intervention:** Spiritual fathers are often available to provide support and care during times of crisis, such as sickness, death, or other difficult situations. The blessing of having a spiritual father is when I was at the point of walking away, he encouraged me to stay.

7. **Pastoral care:** Spiritual fathers offer pastoral care, visit the sick, counsel those in need, and provide comfort and support to their congregation.

8. **Role model:** Spiritual fathers serve as role models for their congregation or spiritual children, demonstrating important values such as compassion, forgiveness, and faith.

9. **Spiritual growth:** A spiritual father plays a crucial role in guiding individuals in their spiritual growth and development. They provide resources, support, and encouragement, paving the way for a deeper connection with their faith.

10. **Connection to a larger faith community:** A spiritual father is not just a leader, but a bridge to a larger faith community. They help connect you to others, fostering a sense of belonging and connection to something greater than yourself. They make you feel valued and part of a community that shares your beliefs and values.

CHAPTER IV

THE ORPHAN SPIRIT

BISHOP RON WEBB'S PERSPECTIVE

The orphan spirit is something that many people suffer with in church and the world. There's something unique about a father's role in a child's life. The father-child relationship is the heart of where our identity is formed and should be a healthy picture of how our Heavenly Father interacts with us. A deep void is created when one is abandoned or rejected by their earthly father. As a result, it is difficult for them to interact with our God. Our trust has been broken and healing must take place.

Someone who has an orphan spirit is a part of a detached entity. The orphan spirit has

- No bloodline
- No birthright
- No inheritance
- No intimacy with the Father

Knowing the Father's love is not just important; it is crucial for a believer to function as a healthy member of the body of Christ. So, what does this spirit look like?

- Sensed abandonment

- Loneliness
- Alienation
- Isolation

Today, we see a multitude of isolated ministers, often leading what they call independent churches. These are not signs of strength, but rather, they are symptoms of the orphan spirit. This spirit breeds dysfunction in our ministries, and it is our responsibility to address it.

SIGNS OF ORPHAN SPIRIT

Ask yourself these questions:
- Do you operate out of insecurity?
- Am I jealous of others' success?
- Do I serve God to earn His love?
- Do I struggle with self-worth?
- Am I driven by the need to succeed?
- Do I use people to accomplish my goals?
- Do I lack self-esteem?

The spirit of adoption is the opposite of the orphan spirit. It is a mindset of security, acceptance, and love that comes from knowing and experiencing the love of our Heavenly Father. When we have the spirit of adoption, we are secure in our relationship with God and our identity as His children. We are able to celebrate the accomplishments of others, serve others, and love ourselves in a healthy way. We are grounded in our identity in Christ and are able to allow the Holy Spirit to lead us into our calling. Overall, the spirit of adoption is characterized by a deep sense of belonging and acceptance in the family of God.

WHEN YOU OPERATE IN A SPIRIT OF ADOPTION

1. You are secure.
2. You celebrate the accomplishments of others.

3. You experience acceptance.
4. You will allow the spirit to lead us into our calling.
5. You serve others.
6. You bless others.
7. You love yourself.
8. You exhibit healthy self-esteem.
9. You are grounded in your identity in Christ.

Jeremiah 29:11 says, "For I know the thoughts that I think toward you, saith the LORD, thoughts of peace, and not of evil, to give you an expected end."

When you pastor a person or train young leaders with an orphan spirit, remember they don't feel accepted and need to prove their worth. They will seek attention from others. Deep down, they don't feel as though they belong in a family, so they develop a spirit or an attitude of independence. This will cause them to be unsure or second-guess themselves. They will always try to prove themselves and become territorial about their ministry areas as they battle with performance issues.

CHAPTER V

SPIRIT OF A BASTARD

BISHOP ADRIAN RODGERS' PERSPECTIVE

The world defines a bastard as an illegitimate child, one born outside of the covenant of marriage or, in this case, without the contract of fatherhood and mentorship.

The Godly definition of bastard is *"But if ye be without chastisement, whereof all are partakers, then are ye bastards, and not sons." Hebrews 12:8 (The King James Version).* The world defines a bastard as a person born out of wedlock, outside the covenant, which parallels to the Godly definition of a bastard, someone that is un-fathered and illegitimate due to lack of spiritual guidance.

Notice in the verse above that those who are willing to be chastised by the Lord are legitimate sons. They yield the peaceable fruit of righteousness in their lives. Those who do not submit to the chastening of the Lord are called bastards. Their fruit is radically different.

One of the dangers of the Bastard spirit is its ability to spread and pollute others. If unmanaged, the bastard spirit can become contagious and draw other bastard spirits. In the Old Testament, the rendering of the Hebrew word "mamzer'," which means "polluted." Polluted -

made unclean or impure; contaminated; tainted. The bastard spirit not only contaminates those it encounters, but it also taints the vision that God has for His church and people.

According to Michael Fackerell, one of the hallmark character-istics of those who have the curse of the bastard in their bloodline is noted in verse 8: they refuse reprimand. They are not teachable, not correctable, and not coachable. They rebel when confronted with correction by anyone exercising legitimate, Godly spiritual author-ity such as a pastor, a husband, or a parent. A person affected by the bastard curse is unwilling to be governed by the Spirit of God. This shows up in their inability to have close fellowship with both the Lord and with fellow believers. Instead, they are often attracted to laws and legalism. They become hardened and easily estranged from fel-low Christians, quickly offended, and unwilling to change focus from themselves and are consumed with the same.

The difference between the sheep and the goats is noticeably clear. The goat is into the self: self-interest, self-gratification, and self-focus. The sheep, on the other hand, are full of compassion. They see the thirsty, the naked, and the hungry. They are not self-focused. Instead they look to help others. When they help, they even forget that they have helped, and they expect nothing in return. While the goat is quick to say, "Look what I did!" a sheep is content to seek neither reputation nor recognition.

Goats in the church call attention to anything good that they do, and quickly forget the evils they do. They also quickly forget the good things that others do for them. This makes it extremely easy for them to say, when a sheep has a need, "Oh, we'll always have hun-gry people around us," or, "If those nations only used birth control, we wouldn't have to deal with so many children." Or, "If you think they need help, then you go help them; I don't want to hear about it (Fackerell, 2004).

I knew a pastor that had a young man who attended his congregation and came from a church run by a board. They did not have a strong Pastor. This young man, whom we will call Doug, never fully submitted to the ministry. He was only focused on himself. Doug came from a failed ministry where seven police cars ended up there on a Sunday morning because of a church fight. He came from an environment that allowed infighting, if the outcome appeared favorable. Doug was gifted musically but refused to work with the music ministry of our church. Although he was invited to be a part of our music department, he chose not to accept the invitation. He did, however, choose to start his own music group with some members of our church on the promise of not missing any services for engagements. Almost immediately that promise was broken.

The members of our church, who were also members of the group, started coming in late or totally missing church. The pastor tried on many levels to work with him. They agreed to four Sundays a year along with many other concessions; however, what he ultimately wanted was to be able to do whatever he wanted to do without consequences or reprimand. Doug was only happy when he was out front in the spotlight. He was not a team player at all. He was a minister in training when he came to the ministry. After only a short while, he asked to be ordained. This was unheard of. The protocol for ministry elevation was for a minister in training to be observed, monitored, and their progress reported. Ministers were to be recommended for elevation; not requested by the trainee. He had only preached twice in the seven years that he had been a member. He did not submit himself fully to regular leadership or ministry training meetings. He was usually noticeably angry with the pastor and his wife, who served as the Co-Pastor of his ministry.

One of the criteria to be in ministry was to operate in the spirit of agreement. His anger was often displayed while the pastor was preaching or teaching. This was not appropriate behavior for a person being considered for ordination. He was disagreeable when asked to perform specific tasks, but critical of those who were placed out front, who agreed with ministry requests. It angered him that the pastor would not ordain him. After not getting what he ultimately desired, which was notoriety and position, he and his wife finally left the ministry. He went on to find another ministry that would quickly ordain him. He displayed the markings of a goat as aforementioned. Sheep submit, while goats rebel.

This young man never had strong male leadership in his life. The young lady that he married had three sons from an earlier relationship. He does not have a good relationship with any of them and his wife has mostly endorsed his behavior. His relationship with her sons, along with her agreement with his behavior, has caused contention with the mother and sons' relationship dynamic. The pastor has observed him deal very harshly with others, while desiring mercy and grace from others. He never embraced the ministry as his spiritual head. He would call someone else his spiritual father, whom he did not have to be accountable to or follow. He is still un-fathered. Men especially need strong male leadership.

CHAPTER VI

NEGATIVE IMPACTS OF ABSENT FATHERS PHYSICALLY AND SPIRITUALLY

BISHOP ADRIAN RODGERS' PERSPECTIVE

Dr. David Popenoe, Professor of Sociology at Rutgers University and Co-Director of the National Marriage Project, has provided us with a good summary and overview of the subject. Here's what he has to say:

Fathers are far more than just "second adults" in the home. Involved fathers – especially biological fathers – bring positive benefits to their children that no other person is as likely to bring. They provide protection, economic support, and male role models. They have a parenting style that is significantly different from that of a mother and that difference is important in healthy child development. - David Popenoe, Life Without Father, (New York: The Free Press, 1996), p. 163.

One of the most vital aspects of a dad's contribution to the lives of his kids lies precisely in what Dr. Popenoe calls his "significantly different parenting style." Men and women are different. As a result, mothers and fathers parent their children differently.

Dads, for instance, love their children "more dangerously." That's because they play "rougher" and are more likely to encourage risk-taking. They provide kids with a broader diversity of social experiences. They also introduce them to a wider variety of methods of dealing with life. They tend to stress rules, justice, fairness, and duty in discipline. In this way, they teach children the objectivity and consequences of right and wrong. They give kids insight into the world of men. They prepare them for the challenges of life and demonstrate by example the meaning of respect between the sexes. In connection with this last point, research indicates that a married father is substantially less likely to abuse his wife or children than men in any other category.

Fathers encourage competition, engendering independence. Mothers promote equity, creating a sense of security. Dads emphasize conceptual communication, which helps kids expand their vocabulary and intellectual capacities. Moms major in sympathy, care, and help, thus demonstrating the importance of relationships. Dads tend to see their child in relation to the rest of the world. Moms tend to see the rest of the world in relation to their child. Neither style of parenting is adequate in and of itself. Taken together, they balance each other out and equip the up-and-coming generation with a healthy, well-rounded approach to life (The Significance Of A Father's Influence, 2011). (Gaille, 2017).

A young man reached out to a pastor I know on social media and said that he needed to be fathered. I knew him as a musician and later learned that he was also a preacher. This young man grew up in a church where the Pastor was very flawed. In fact, a few years ago this Pastor was murdered and the facts that came out were unfortunate concerning him. He later moved to Memphis and bounced around to several ministries. Due to his talent and ability, he had no problem finding a church to play for. He would play the organ at this place a while and then go on to somewhere else; however, he did not seem to connect anywhere. He now belonged to a church that did not require accountability and felt that he needed more. He told the pastor that he wanted someone who would hold him accountable and be the spiritual father that he needed.

After several conversations, he joined the church at the end of Bible Study on a Tuesday night. After joining, he came back one or two times and then disappeared. At first, he would text or answer the pastor's phone calls, but he would offer flimsy excuses. After that, nothing! The next thing I knew, he started calling himself Prophet and holding Sunday night services in various locations. These were not word-based services; they were filled with mostly prophesying and dancing. Somebody uncovered and not planted was now trying to lead others. Since he was talented as a musician and preacher and had a prophetic gift and charisma, people were following him. How do you lead people when you have not been properly led? How do you expect people to be consistent, dedicated, and faithful when you have not been? Basically, this young man floats to any new fellowship or group that springs up, looking for a position and affirmation. He is now pastoring a church.

The Bible says in *Galatians 6:7 (The King James Version), "⁷ Be not deceived; God is not mocked: for whatsoever a man soweth, that shall he also reap."* An unplanted and unstable Pastor will draw un-planted and unstable people. A church started with the expectation of prophecy only--not soul-winning, and spiritual maturity-- will always have people, but not the same people. People will slide in and out looking for "A WORD" instead of growing in the "The Word."

CHAPTER VII

HOW SOCIETY, CULTURE, CHURCHES, EDUCATION, FAMILIES, AND INDIVIDUALS ARE AFFECTED AND INFECTED

BISHOP ADRIAN RODGERS' PERSPECTIVE

Recently, the federal government released its latest figures on births in the United States, including out-of-wedlock births. The numbers are very close to last year's:

- 72.3 percent of non-Hispanic blacks are now born out-of-wedlock;
- 66.2 percent of American Indians/Alaska Natives;
- 53.3 percent of Hispanics;
- 29.1 percent of non-Hispanic whites;
- and 17.2 percent of Asians/Pacific Islanders.

That's 40.7 percent overall: a disaster. It is, of course, no surprise that the groups with the highest illegitimacy rates are the groups that are struggling economically, educationally, and socially, just to name a few (Gaille, 2017).

On May 25, 2017, Brandon Gaille published an article called 29 Enticing Illegitimate Children Statistics. He mentions how every child deserves a chance to be loved and to follow their dreams. Children can enter into this world into a wide variety of family environments. With the increase of cohabitation in relation to marriage, however, the amount of children who fill up the illegitimate birth statistics is beginning to rise. In the United States, over 40% of the total births that occur annually are considered illegitimate births (Gaille, 2017).

When children lack the parental structure of a father in the home, it is easy for the children to fantasize about the life they thought they would have had. In the land of imagination, any scenario is possible. A father you imagine can fit any profile you desire. Imaginations, like memories, are not reliable. There is no perfect natural parent; they do not exist. The only perfect parent is Jehovah God.

Yes, "A REAL FATHER" will be there for you. He will attend your birthday parties, graduations, piano or dance recitals, church/school plays, and any other activities. He will be there to assure you that your first pimple is not the end of your life, to hug you, kiss you and call you by his favorite pet name for you. However, A REAL FATHER must also correct you, discipline you, and tell you "no" sometimes. It cannot always be peaches and cream. The Bible says in *Hebrews 12:7 KJV, "If ye endure chastening, God dealeth with you as with sons; for what son is he whom the father chasteneth not?"* Also, *Proverbs 3:12 KJV, "For whom the LORD loveth he correcteth; even as a father the son in whom he delighteth."*

Many are accustomed to the correction and love of a mother because they have experience with it. However, the correction and love of a father is foreign to them. Additionally, many were corrected by a frustrated mother who had to do all the parenting alone. Regardless of how society tries to paint it, it is hard to bring home the bacon and fry it up in the pan. So, any correction outside of the familiar is viewed as negative.

These sinful actions of having sex outside of marriage and bringing children into single parent homes have made situations chaotic in our world. Children of all ages have imaginations of the love of their birth fathers. Children that were once young are adults now and still have fantasies of what a father's love should look like. It causes them to have unrealistic expectations of every man who enters their lives, including, but not limited to, husbands, pastors, and employers. These unrealistic expectations cause undue pressure for those males who love them. It is impossible to live up to the expectations of someone who relies only on their imagined reality and have never bothered to share their expectations with the person they are expecting to fulfill them. What are some examples of unrealistic expectations?

1. He will never disappoint me.
2. He will only tell me what I want to hear.
3. He will always give me what I want and when I want it.
4. He will always say yes.
5. He will always give me his undivided attention.
6. He will never correct me only compliment me.

Whenever the males in their lives offer correction or point out what is not a flattering personal characteristic, they will quickly hear, "YOU'RE NOT MY DADDY" OR "YOU CAN'T TELL ME WHAT TO DO." The husband may get the cold shoulder in the bedroom. The other male figures may feel the LOUD SILENCE, BE IGNORED, or experience a TANTRUM or even TEARS.

CHAPTER VIII

THE DANGER OF ALLOWING BASTARDS IN THE PULPIT

BISHOP ADRIAN RODGERS' PERSPECTIVE

The Bible says in *Hebrews 12:8 (The King James Version)*, *"But if ye be without chastisement, whereof all are partakers, then are ye bastards, and not sons."* Some who have given their hearts to the Lord have never experienced true deliverance. They have experienced salvation from sin, but not from their past. They are saved, but they still struggle with instructions, and any kind of corrections. They only want compliments and affirmation, but no constructive criticism. Our lives must be balanced! Nobody, absolutely nobody, gets it right all the time. So, for that reason, there are times of praise and times of constructive criticism.

Ecclesiastes 3:1 (The King James Version) says, "To everything there is a season, and a time to every purpose under the heaven."

There are times and seasons for everything. Just like there are times to compliment, there are also times to be corrected and constructively criticized. The definition of correction is 1: the action or an instance of correcting, such as a: AMENDMENT, RECTIFICATION

b: REBUKE, PUNISHMENT

c: a bringing into conformity with a standard

To fix is not to embarrass or to destroy. It is merely to correct a wrong action or behavior, to bring into conformity with a standard. You cannot live life expecting to do whatever you want to do without consequence. You do not want to live that kind of life. When you are out of order, it should be your ultimate desire to be brought back into alignment. The Bible says *"Let all things be done decently and in order. You do not want to reap the disaster of an out of order life."* 1 *Corinthians 14:40 (The King James Version).*

Constructive criticism is needed in all our lives. Notice the definition of constructive: promoting improvement or development. The description of "criticize" is to find fault with or point out the faults of. So constructive criticism means to promote improvement or development by pointing out faults. This is not to tear anyone down but to build them up. A good father always wants to pull the best out of you. He wants you to be your absolute best. The danger of the population of bastards in the pulpit exposed the kingdom of God to men and women, who may be called to pulpit ministry and influence. However, the platform given has been polluted by the absence of discipline and reprimand. This behavior opens the church up to the harvest of this cyclic behavior. Someone must recognize the danger, cry aloud, and provide assistance to clean up what has become contaminated.

Currently, we, as a society, are exposed to a disease that has reached epidemic proportions. One of the dangers of this disease besides not having a vaccination to prevent the spread of the disease is not being able to contain exposure or narrow its effects altogether. The condition shows up in everyone differently, mimicking a chameleon disease. The symptoms are widespread, affecting all nationalities, creeds, and age groups. While many have survived the disease, several have succumbed to its inevitable end. Similarly, the undisciplined, tainted that reach the pulpit spread the infection of being a spiritual bastard without totally being aware that they are diseased. The Word of God is the vaccination for our spiritual and social ills. God's word is the mirror by which all men must measure the status of their souls.

The Word of God, however, has been placed in the hands of imperfect humanity. It warns us of misinterpreting its value and meaning, causing men to be led astray. Every person, good or bad, has a sphere of influence. The Bible gives us examples in the lives of the sects that arose from the 400 silent years. The Sadducees, Pharisees, and the Sanhedrin Council were Jewish religious leaders who vehemently stood in the convicted belief that they were upholding Jewish law. Jesus came into these times and stood as the incarnate Christ, declaring the truth of the Word. This truth challenged the religious leaders of His day. We are challenged during this time to do the same. The danger of the un-pastored is how they will pass their skewed views to others who will repeat the same cycles. Just as our nation is currently trying to contain the pandemic and limit its reach, the called-out ones must find and father the un-fathered.

Those called to be Pastors and ministers cannot endure the ministerial journey alone. It is very dangerous for those in ministry to be un-fathered and to forge ahead into ministry without a spiritual father. To go at it alone causes destruction and much uncertainty (Rudnick, 2014). For example, a pastor called me on the phone one day several years ago. He had seen our church website and had questions about the ministry. He told me that he was from another state and that he had a great ministry there. He also stated that he had a sister in Jonesboro and would be coming to visit her soon.

A few months later, he came to Jonesboro and we met. In a matter of weeks, he was starting a church in Jonesboro. In my mind, I was thinking what happened to the great church you said you had out of state? I was asked to come and preach at the new church and agreed to do so. The pastor told me he was having services in a garage. I thought he meant that a repair garage had been converted into a church building. When we pulled up to the address, it was a residential address. I had a van and several vehicles following me to a house! My wife, who was not feeling well, looked at me and said, "I am going home." We had to go through the house to get to the garage. Shocked beyond words, we walked past a naked baby, a family watching television and smoking marijuana. When we got into the garage, it was fully set up with church furnishings, pews, pulpit, communion table, and kneeling altar, from the "great church" in another state.

A year went by, and he invited me to come again, informing me that he had moved into a rental facility. I went along with several members from our church. The service was very unorganized and poorly attended by those he said he led. I have known this individual probably for 15 years. In that amount of time, he has moved at least ten times or more and has started more than 15 churches; some he pastored himself and others he has put other ministers over. No matter how great the failure or how great the loss, when this young man fails, he moves and starts all over again because he only wants to lead and not follow. He wants to father others and not accept the benefit of being fathered. One day the pastor decided to show me his credentials, and honestly, he should not have. Some were hand-written, and all were of poor quality, evidently created by others who should have been followers and not leaders as well.

CHAPTER IX

THE DANGER OF BEING WITHOUT A FATHER SPIRITUALLY

BISHOP ADRIAN RODGERS' PERSPECTIVE

A man or woman entering ministry should certainly already be an active member of a church and submitted to the Pastor. The reasons to preach should be to spread the gospel, see souls saved and help to mature the saints, not to simply to tell people off and get things off your chest. A time of preparation is best served under the tutelage of your Pastor or whoever he has assigned to that area of teaching or mentorship. It is imperative that as your ministry begins to grow, and your popularity begins to expand, that you remain humble. Humility is an area where many falter. When people receive several public accolades, it is easy to get lifted in pride and begin to think that any correction is out of jealousy or feelings of intimidation.

True spiritual correction comes from a pure place of assistance. I know there have been occasions where jealousy or feelings of intimidation may have been involved, but real called pastors only want to help. They know the dangers and pitfalls that others outside of that calling are not aware of and have not encountered. My spiritual father is also my natural father, Bishop Charles Rodgers. He has been in active, preaching ministry since he was 14 years old and at the time of this thesis, he is 78 years old. His instructions saved me from many pitfalls. I have had my share of them, but I was spared from many more. The pitfalls I avoided are largely due to his mentorship and guidance. Those without a healthy father-son dynamic, may consider my respect for him to be overboard or excessive. Caution, however, mixed with wisdom is a recipe for unnecessary mistakes. For instance, whenever I received an invitation to preach, I never accepted it until I spoke with him. Most of the time he approved, but occasionally he would say, "I don't think you should accept the engagement." Sometimes he explained why, and other times, he simply said, "Trust me on this one." There are times I found out later that the ministry that sent the invitation or the pastor of the church had a bad reputation or may have mistreated me in some manner. It is so important to listen to the one you are submitted and assigned to.

Please know that there are no overnight sensations in ministry that have lasting tenure. I know that there are people that we didn't know previously in kingdom ministry that seemed to have come out of nowhere. However, when you learn their history, you will usually find that they spent many years behind the scenes. They were preaching in the small places, serving their pastors, and doing the seemingly menial tasks, wondering all the while if they would ever make it. Bishop T.D. Jakes, one of the most recognized preachers in America, was preaching and pastoring many, many years before most of the world ever heard of him. From the hills of W. Virginia, he was sitting in the Azusa Conference in the upper balcony, when someone suggested to Bishop Carlton Pearson, the conference host, that he should hear Bishop Jakes' minister. He followed their advice. This put Bishop Jakes on a national platform, catapulting him into public ministry. Now there is hardly anywhere he can go, in the states or abroad, where he is not recognized. This very day Bishop Jakes was on national news speaking to America about protests and riots that are going on. This is the same preacher that was pastoring a very small church in obscurity. He was anointed by God but struggling. He was used by God, but seemingly spinning his wheels. Now millions and millions of people know his name. He is the Founder and Senior Pastor of The Potter's House Church in Dallas, TX with a confirmed flock exceeding 30,000 parishioners.

In the words of the man I used to work for, Bob Hazard, "You must be careful not to start believing all of your own press." Believing your own press means you should not believe only the good thoughts you think of yourself. It is important to have people in your life to keep you balanced and accurate. The Bible says in *Luke 6:26 (KJV)*, *"Woe unto you, when all men shall speak well of you! for so did their fathers to the false prophets."* When your head begins to swell from the compliments of others, it can alter your ability to hear clearly. For example, a pastor friend of mine shared that at the age of twenty-one, he was advised to take a church as pastor. Those that advised him considered themselves as spiritual fathers, but only gave advice based on what was best for their group of peers at that time.

He took a church of 35 members in a rural area of Arkansas. He was an evangelist, happy and fulfilled in his calling. He was married for two years with a new 4-month-old baby, and peers began saying, "You need to stop evangelizing and pastor a church." They told him he had a family and the road life was not a good life for a family. With no spiritual father and no fivefold teaching or training, it sounded logical, so he and his wife took the church as pastor. The members loved them and followed them immediately.

His heart was still evangelism, so he continued to travel and evangelize. He made an attempt to pastor without any training, help, or preparation. The church grew in five months to over 100, and within one year, over 150 members. At that point, he had a congregation that needed a pastor, a shepherd and he was not prepared, nor qualified. As he continued to evangelize, he would call in pastors to preach for him and help with issues in the church. However, most of those he used, saw it as an opportunity to disqualify him to his congregation, and some even tried to take over the ministry. He began to take it all personal. His hurt turned to anger, anger to bitterness, and bitterness turned to a heart of stone.

The church was continuing to grow. The people began to see their frailties. An opportunity for control of the church and the pastor began to take place. My friend fought it for a while. With no spiritual father to turn to, he sought an overseer in an organization, that advised him to leave and start over in another church. Instead, he resigned because his heart was not right. He had grown cold. Therefore, he walked away from it all.

His decision resulted in many mistakes and failures for himself and his family. His decision caused the church to split and those that remained were down to less than twenty within a few months. For over a year, he worked with churches in music departments but would not do anything he was called to do. Then he met a Pastor who reached out to him, loved him, restored him, restored his faith, and became a Real Spiritual father to him. He served under him for over fifteen years, learning, growing and returning to evangelizing with his family.

His spiritual father taught him how to operate under the fivefold ministry. He finally had someone who would love, guide, correct and impart. He connected him to other leaders, fathers and mothers in the gospel. The spiritual father was so confident in his God inspired assignment towards my friend, that he was not intimidated by the addition of other leaders in his life. My friend communicated things would have been different if he first had a spiritual father.

Just as my friend benefitted from correction, so did I while working for The Keyboard Place in Memphis, TN. Whenever I made a big sale, I would want to talk about it, I would want to brag about it but the owner would say, "Great job but that sale is over. It's time to start working on the next one." In fact, it was the last secular job I held before God called me into fulltime ministry. I learned several life lessons during my tenure there. I was a young man when I started. I was someone brash and even a little overzealous. I learned the value of teamwork. This was the first job in management that I ever held. But it was not immediate; I had to come up the ranks. I had to learn how to work in corporate America. I had been in leadership in the church since my early teens. This was a different and necessary experience. I would have the garner the respect of my peers, submit to higher management and learn to function at every level of the company.

Before I became a manager, I remember the owner, Mr. Hazard, doubling my responsibilities and applying pressure to me in ways he had not previously. I was perplexed by his actions, but I did not feel as though I needed to ask what was going on. So, I persevered, but at one point, I told my wife that I thought I was being set up too. After several weeks of what I later learned was intense training, Mr. Hazard called me in and told me that he had secretly been testing me to see if I could handle the responsibility of management. Mr. Hazard was one of those who taught me the value of discipline and long-range goals. He and a partner started the company and it became a thriving business. I learned the value of correction. Because this was a sales and commission job, my ability to receive correction affected my income. So, I quickly learned how to take correction that I did not always agree with because my mentor had a proven record of accomplishment. Mentors and fathers come in all forms. Mr. Hazard was like a father to me. His training proved invaluable. Even after I left the job, the owner would call me back to booster certain sales promotions. We have remained close until now. Many of the lessons I learned there have even transferred into ministry.

One of the most important lessons is to learn that life lessons are built upon what was learned from the former lesson. The mentor or spiritual parent is partly responsible for continued progress. One success or even multiple successes are not a reason to rest or delay advancement. Resting on your laurels keeps you from moving forward. My Father used to say, "Good is the enemy of better, better is the enemy of best and best is the enemy of greater." A good parent, coach, employer, or pastor is ALWAYS pushing you forward, which means they will not consistently allow you to talk about what you used to do or your previous accomplishments. They are not trying to diminish those things; they just do not want your looking back to hinder you from moving forward.

A car has a large windshield, but a small rearview mirror because moving forward is what you really want to do. The rearview mirror is to help you when you are momentarily in reverse. It is also to assist you in not making mistakes while moving forward. The rearview mirrors in our lives are to teach us how to avoid the errors of our past. For the Christian believer, this means employing the Holy Spirit and the Bible to prevent going backwards and provoke a hopeful future. One of the practices of a Christian believer is prayer. Prayer keeps the flesh out of ministry. The flesh will cause you to focus on previous successes and impede present and future goals. Flesh is always waiting to creep in, no matter how anointed and gifted you are. If left unchecked, flesh will creep in. That is why there is such a spirit of arrogance and pride among some in ministry now because flesh has crept in. The scripture teaches us in *Philippians 3:13-14 (The King James Version), "Brethren, I count not myself to have apprehended:*

but this one thing I do, forgetting those things which are behind, and reaching forth unto those things which are before, [14] I press toward the mark for the prize of the high calling of God in Christ Jesus."

CHAPTER X

TRANSITIONING FROM THE UN-FATHERED TO THE FATHERED

BISHOP ADRIAN RODGERS' PERSPECTIVE

In my experience as being a pastor, I quickly understood that the same way my father served as a natural and spiritual father to many, along with other men of God, my calling as a pastor would allow me to become a spiritual father to the others. We will now hear from 3 parishioners from my congregation that discuss their transition from un-fathered to fathered in both a natural and spiritual sense.

CHRISTY'S VIEW: THE IMPACT OF DAD VS SPIRITUAL FATHER

It is my belief that the correlation between an earthly father's relationship emphatically impacts the foundational relationship that one has with Father God. For this reason, it has been most profitable for me to have a spiritual father in my life, one who makes up the difference. This is my account of Fatherly Impacts both paternal/biological and spiritual.

The impact of fatherhood in my life is not at all subjective, but an objective and a well-documented phenomenon. My biological father and my mother were never married but they were in a very serious relationship (according to both of their accounts). From infancy throughout my teenage years, my biological father was absent. Communication was rare, so fatherly validation was just a fairytale; emotional support was obsolete; financial contributions were nonexistent; broken promises were the norm; rejection was my reality. As far as I can remember, I was plagued with father hunger, lacking the sufficiency of absolute protection, security, love, and affirmation that I so needed. I had a wonderful mother who provided her best, but the best mother did not have enough to complete the package. I was raised in a God-fearing home, where I was taught that Jesus was the answer to everything, and I believed that. However, in the back of my mind, I could not give Him/Jesus/God every part of me because He was The Father and to me, fathers disappoint. So subconsciously, my relationship with my biological father impacted my relationship with who I now know as ABBA.

At 17 years old, a recent high school graduate and now an away from home college freshman, I began to venture out on my own. During my second semester at Arkansas State University, I became increasingly intrigued by this ministry that harped on deliverance, wholeness, the Love of God, and Spiritual son-ship. The Pastor was so involved in teaching practical biblical principles and life application that I was awed. He was much like what I pictured a good natural father would be with their children, but he was doing it through the word and to his entire flock. As I submitted to his teachings, I began to see changes in my life. I became a vested, active member of the church and a devout follower of Christ. A father is a teacher; a teacher through example, rebuke, encouragement, love and deed. Bishop Adrian Rodgers had begun to father me. It was uncomfortable and yet endearing at the same time. Being fathered was uncomfortable because I'd never experienced it in wholeness. It was endearing be-cause internally it was exactly what I had always yearned for. Finally, I started to feel "covered" which is synonymous with protected.

When we are biologically young, we need our parents to teach us how to walk, talk, feed, bathe, and care for ourselves in every other way. Basically, our human parents are intended to be a PHYSICAL covering for us in every area while we are growing up. Similarly, this is what I found in Bishop Adrian, a covering for me in every area spiritually. Through his teaching, I was taught how to walk as a Christian, how to feed myself through the study of God's word, how to bathe and cleanse through repentance, how to love others even those who hurt me, and even my biological father. The things that I was lacking with my biological father, Bishop Adrian Rodgers, my spiritual father, had begun to fill. He watched over me and covered me in prayer. I was no longer vulnerable. I was protected. He saw treasure in me, spoke into my life, building me up and encouraging me to be all Christ made me to be; I felt affirmed. Bishop Adrian gave me opportunities to practice what I'm called to do, which forced me to grow. I felt esteemed and confident. He rebuked, disciplined and counseled me when needed. I knew I was loved. Where I once had no male authority, I now had a role model and godly example to pattern my life after. I'd gained a spiritual inheritance. I've profited from his hard work, receiving some skills, anointing, networks and relation-ships, not because I've earned them but because he did. I'm just in position as a son (daughter) to receive it.

Being afforded many of the aforementioned things through my spiritual father gave me grace for my natural father, which fostered healing and restoration in that relationship. Not only did having a spiritual father enhance my biological relationship, but it also gave me renewed confidence in ABBA. I was taught that man is faulty (even spiritual authority), but Christ/ABBA is ABSOLUTE. My faith in FATHERHOOD is restored.

CARLA'S VIEW: THE DIFFERENCE HAVING A SPIRITUAL FATHER MADE...

I have always known "who" my father (biological) was and where he was. However, our time together has been so scattered and sporadic throughout my 44 years, that a genuine father/daughter relationship has been inevitably, non-existent.

As any daughter would, I needed a father; I longed to be a "Daddy's girl." However, that was not my initial reality. For me, the detrimental effects of not having a father in my life yielded some very catastrophic issues throughout my latter teens and young adult life. It set the stage for REJECTION, LOW SELF ESTEEM, ANGER, BITTERNESS, RESENTMENT, and FEAR; all emotions that I experienced for many years.

Fast forward to 1995; I was 19 years old and was completing my Freshman year of college at Arkansas State University. Because I didn't love myself, or know who I was, I accepted anything that I felt accepted me; good or bad. I was filled with anger and rage, which came out in many situations where I felt "my security" was at stake. I fought a lot... I was lost and I was searching for all the things that I lacked: love, security, acceptance and validation. College eventually became too overwhelming for me, and soon I lost my academic scholarship and was put out of college two years later.

Around this time, I met Pastor and Co-Pastor Adrian & Susan Rodgers, a nice couple from my hometown. I didn't really care for Pastor Rodgers initially (LOL). He was too direct and outspoken, so I thought. I felt like he was intrusive, and I did not understand his level of "being in your business;" (ahh, the characteristics of a Dad). After getting to know them, I eventually became a member of Fullness of Joy Ministries, and they took on the daunting task of becoming my spiritual parents. As our relationship began to flourish, I began to understand that I had been given a chance to go back to those formative years and "pick up the little girl who was dropped" and begin the healing process.

I do not have adequate space to entail everything that I learned or gained with our relationship, but I can say that as a father figure, Adrian Rodgers helped to save my life. He restored my faith in fathers/men and modeled the true and extensive love of a father. In a span of 25 years (1995-2020), I can see the difference of having a spiritual father in my life.

With the consistency of a loving and supportive father figure, along with sound teaching of God's word, my life did a complete 180! Today, I celebrate being an overcomer! I am not the broken little girl who once expressed herself through anger and fighting. I recovered from having a child out of wedlock. I stayed and fought for a marriage that I thought was heading towards divorce. I went back to the same university that I was kicked out of and obtained 3 degrees (Bachelor's, Master's and Specialist's). I have now been married for 21 years, and we have raised two remarkable young men: one who recently graduated from Vanderbilt University and one who is headed to SCAD (Savannah College of Art & Design) in the fall. I am a homeowner, a successful and dedicated educator, a mentor, a spiritual mother to others, a new business owner and I have broken MANY generational curses.

My life has been enriched because of the presence of my spiritual father. He has been there for every high and low that I have experienced in life. He has celebrated and chastised me. He has taught me the importance of forgiving those who "dropped the ball in my life." So today, I stand tall in forgiveness, joy, and peace because of the many things that my spiritual father instilled in me throughout the past 25 years. Adrian Rodgers is MY proof that GOD LOVES ME and that He didn't forget about me!

CHRIS' VIEW: THE IMPACT OF DAD VS. SPIRITUAL FATHER

Growing up, a present father in the home was rare. Fortunately, I had mine. He took his role very seriously. He provided, supported, disciplined, and gave guidance the best he knew how. He modeled and exemplified love, not only for his children but for the community. Those who didn't have fathers could call him dad because he made sure those who were hungry ate. He made sure they had clothes and somewhere safe to sleep. He taught them as he taught us.

There were times we wondered why he made such a sacrifice, spending what we considered "all our money" to help others. We, as children, thought about all of the additional things we could have if he did not take care of so many others. He taught us the importance of giving. He was a very selfless and loving man. My father gave me everything he could to ensure I was strong, self-sufficient, loving, a good husband, and a good father.

My father realized there was more that I needed. More that he struggled to give me because of the life he was forced to live during the Vietnam War. Though his actions were to survive, they tore at his heart and drove a mental wedge between him and God. So, in spiritual manners, he would only go so far. However, he was fully aware that I was different and needed something more than what he was able to offer. Being a man's man who absolutely loved his assignment to father, he struggled with the thought of another man fathering me. As he began to see my spiritual growth, he blessed my relationship with my spiritual father.

The same lessons and experiences I was afforded from my father, in the natural, were the lessons and experiences I was longing for in the spirit. My spiritual father pours into me that which my biological father was unable to. Every lesson learned from my biological father is being taught from Christ's perspective by my spiritual father. My father, Larry, taught me how to love as a man. My spiritual father, Adrian, teaches me how a man should love according to the word of God. Where my father taught me the importance of wealth, my spiritual father taught me about stewardship and giving, sowing and reaping, tithing and offering. My father, Larry, taught me to be a man's man and to walk with boldness and confidence. My spiritual father, Adrian, taught me to walk in holy boldness, confidence and full spiritual authority.

All in all, like my biological father, my spiritual father takes his role in my life seriously. Spiritually, he provides, supports, disciplines, and gives guidance the best he knows how. Being led by the Word of God, he models and exemplifies God's love, not only for his spiritual sons and daughters but for those in the community who do not have spiritual fathers. Many call him dad because he makes sure those who are hungry are fed the word of God. He teaches them as he teaches us.

His role in my life is just as important as the role my biological father served in. There is now balance in my life because I have had the honor of being fathered by two great men who took and continue to take their roles seriously.

Spiritual parenting is a rewarding assignment; however it is not an easy task. Just as it often takes years for natural children to understand that their parents are not their enemies, it parallels similarly in the spirit. You can see what God is trying to do in the lives of those you parent and mentor. You may even hear from the Lord specifically as to your assignment in their lives. However, just as Elijah was called to mentor and mold Elisha, the child is not always privy to the plan and direction of God. Truly, even if the child is aware, it does not always make the assignment any easier.

Parenting can be hurtful to the parent and the child. Hurtful, in that even though you know in your heart, the decision you are making is the right thing to do, it does not always alleviate the pain of requiring change where one is comfortable or complacent.

When one does not have the advantage of a natural father, as mentioned in the two accounts of some of my members, it is quite difficult to make them understand or even have peace with the markings of fatherhood and authority. Authority is generally resented without a relationship. But relationships take time, trust takes even longer. Our trust in the omniscient God is tested with time and experience. God has a proven track record, but we are not without challenges because He is trustworthy. We KNOW He will bring us out and through our difficulties, trust, however, is required when we don't exactly know HOW He will do that. If it takes time with God, imagine the challenges of a mentor and spiritual father.

There are times of awkwardness, mistrust, defiance, and silence to name a few. A spiritual father has to weather the storms of their own life, while assisting others with theirs. Again, it is not just the responsibility of the father to parent, but the spiritual children to trust and obey.

CHAPTER XI

TEST THEM BEFORE YOU TAG THEM

<u>BISHOP RON WEBB'S PERSPECTIVE</u>

It is important that before a product is branded or tagged, it is tested first. I remember that some years ago, there was an old TV commercial about a certain brand. The commercial emphasized how the quality must go into the product before the name goes on. Another example is the automobile industry. For instance, Ram Tough is mentioned at the end of a Dodge truck commercial. There's the demonstration of the products as you see the driver of the truck driving through a rough terrain up and down a steep hill filled with rocks. You may see a battering ram beating against a wall. Afterward, a sticker price is placed on the window as it is being tagged.

Products are tested before they are labeled (tagged) through a series of quality control measures. Manufacturers ensure that their products meet certain standards and specifications before they are released to the market. Testing may involve physical and chemical analyses of the product, as well as assessment of its performance, safety, and reliability. These tests are designed to identify any defects, flaws, or weaknesses in the product, so that they can be addressed before it is labeled and sold to consumers. The goal is to ensure that the product is of high quality and meets the expectations of customers.

Now, if that happens in the secular world, how much more should we, as Christians, be more alert when it comes to testing people for a leadership position? So we must establish before you're tagged to lead, which means officially recognized and appointed, and ensure you're a faithful follower.

You must always test their ability to serve before you promote them as a successor. Make sure they have put their time in and pass the sacrifice test. Notice how, in the Book of Exodus and the Book of Numbers, Joshua served Moses for many years. Joshua was Moses' assistant and played a vital role in the Israelites' journey to the Promised Land. He was chosen by Moses to lead the Israelites after his death, and Joshua proved to be a faithful and capable leader. He also undergirded him. He fought with him and he fought for him. Then, later on, God speaks to Moses to bring Joshua forth. Notice it was after the fact that he had served and supported him. This biblical example underscores the importance of testing and serving before promoting to leadership roles.

TEST PEOPLE BEFORE YOU TAG THEM.

Pastor, remember, it's crucial to never place individuals in positions of authority if they haven't first experienced the humility of serving. In our power-driven world, where the desire for status often outweighs patience, it's important to resist this urge and wait for the right time, which means waiting until the individual has demonstrated the necessary qualities and readiness for the leadership role. Please understand your wait is not a waste, but a necessary part of the process to ensure the right person is in the right position at the right time.

People can be power-hungry when they have a strong desire for control and authority over others. They may seek positions of power or influence in order to fulfill their own personal desires, rather than seeking to serve others. This can lead to a lack of concern for the well-being of others, as well as a disregard for the values and principles that should guide their decision-making. This kind of behavior can be harmful both to individuals and to society as a whole. Therefore, the consequences of not testing individuals before promoting them can be detrimental to the ministry and its mission.

David served as a shepherd at Jesse's house, attending sheep (1 Samuel 16). He was faithful there and then later on, he was promoted again over Hebron (2 Samuel 2). Later in life, he was anointed over all of Israel. David was a man of great faith and trust in God, as evidenced by his many psalms and prayers. Even when he made mistakes, he always turned back to God and repented. His faithfulness and obedience to God are what made him a great leader and king in Israel's history. Each time he's proven on every level. Similarly, Joseph was tested through his experiences in Potiphar's house and in prison before being promoted to a position of leadership in Egypt.

Pastor, don't just promote people to be faithful. Promote them because they are faithful. Faithful in serving, faithful in giving. Don't make the mistake of tagging, promoting, recommending, and endorsing them if they don't pass the faithful test. If they only want your influence and connections, make them wait and let there be a proven season. By promoting individuals based on their faithfulness, you inspire others to prioritize the right values and to strive for true leadership, not just a title.

Some characteristics of someone a pastor should promote in ministry are faithfulness, humility, servant-heartedness, a teachable spirit, a willingness to learn and grow, a good reputation, and a passion for the vision and mission of the ministry. These individuals are usually reliable and trustworthy, have a positive attitude and work ethic, and are dedicated to serving others. They also have a good understanding of the ministry's values, goals, and strategies, and can effectively communicate and implement them. To test these qualities, you can observe their interactions with others, review their past actions and decisions, and ask for feedback from those they have served or worked with.

You can wait on the blessing or you can try to force the hand of your leadership. Notice none of the proteges demanded a position, promotion or to be the next in line. They waited until the right door opened.

CHAPTER XII

THE DANGER OF SELF-PROMOTION

BISHOP RON WEBB'S PERSPECTIVE

We live in a power-hungry, position-seeking world. Self-promotion is probably one of humanity's most destructive pursuits. There are many examples of people being power-hungry and position-seeking in the world. Some individuals may resort to unethical or even illegal means to achieve their desired level of power and influence. For instance, a politician may employ corrupt tactics to win an election and gain control over a region. Similarly, a business executive may use their position of authority to manipulate their subordinates for their own benefit. Even in everyday life, people may engage in power struggles to gain control over a situation or assert their dominance over others. Ultimately, this kind of behavior can lead to a toxic and unstable environment, where trust is eroded, and relationships are damaged. Many scriptures warn us against it.

Proverb 25:6-7 says, "⁶ Put not forth thyself in the presence of the king, and stand not in the place of great men:⁷ For better it is that it be said unto thee, Come up hither; than that thou shouldest be put lower in the presence of the prince whom thine eyes have seen."

Scripture from Genesis to Revelation reminds us that Jesus mentioned in his earthly ministry that *whoever exalts himself will be abased or humbled, but whoever humbles himself will be exalted (Matthew 23:13, Luke 14:11, 18:14).*

And then we're reminded once again not to think of oneself more *highly than you ought to (Romans 12:3-8);* you don't have to tute your own horn.

Proverbs 27:2 says, "Let another man praise thee, and not thine own mouth; a stranger, and not thine own lips."

Indeed the desire to seek great things for one's self emanates from the devil himself.

Isaiah 14:13 says, "For thou hast said in thine heart, I will ascend into heaven, I will exalt my throne above the stars of God: I will sit also upon the mount of the congregation, in the sides of the north:"

By this thought alone, he was ousted from heaven in a great war (Rev. 12:10).

The Bible says a *man can receive nothing except it be given him from above (John 3:27).*

Remember, *promotion cometh neither from the south, east, west, but from above (Psalm 75:6).*

Anytime you see people fighting over being appointed or trying to self-promote, it's a bad sign that they are headed for swift destruction.

Let's examine Genesis 11, where we are told of men who wanted to build a tower that reached up to the heavens. Now, building a tower building, a house, a business, or a family is fine. We must remember that God checks out our motives or reasons for doing what we do, our desires, and our will. Their reasons for building wasn't to glorify God. It was to make a name for themselves. It was a big mistake because *except the Lord builds the house your labor is in vain (Psalm 127:1).*

There are so many social media platforms today that you can't keep up with them. People use social media to promote themselves in various ways such as posting pictures or videos of themselves show-casing their talents, sharing their achievements, highlighting their skills, flaunting their possessions, and so on. They also use social media to create a persona or brand image that they want others to as-sociate them with. Some people even buy followers or likes to make themselves seem more popular or influential than they actually are. However, it is important to remember that true success and recog-nition come from God, hard work, dedication, and humility rather than just seeking attention or fame on social media. It's all about self-promotion, so people are *building their houses upon sand rather than rock (Matthew 7:24-27).*

Let us delve into the story of Absalom, a figure we encounter in 2 Samuel 18:18. In his quest for recognition and power, Absalom, the son of David, erected a monument to himself. His ambition was not only to gain prominence but also to usurp his father's throne. This act of self-aggrandizement serves as a cautionary tale, reminding us of the perils of self-centered motives.

DANGER OF SELF-PROMOTION

Absalom positioned himself as a people's man. He was a mas-ter manipulator, undermining David's leadership to gain the favor of people by stroking their egos and licking their wounds. There are people who will promote themselves because they are tired of waiting to be promoted by an individual or an organization.

- Self-promotion can lead to a lack of credibility and trust among peers and potential clients.
- It can also create an inflated sense of self-importance, which can lead to a failure to listen to others or take constructive criticism.
- Additionally, self-promotion can create a negative reputation, causing others to view the self-promoter as arrogant, selfish, or insincere.
- Finally, self-promotion can lead to burnout, as individuals who constantly tout their accomplishments can become consumed with the need to maintain a certain image, rather than focusing on their work or personal growth.

I have had many say to me that they felt left out, overlooked, unnoticed, unliked, and unappreciated, so they decided to promote themselves. They went on the internet and ordered their ordination papers. They never had hands laid on them or the approval of their leader, pastor, bishop overseer, or overseer. Remember, promotion comes from above.

So, then, what was Absalom's outcome? Of course, he self-destructed. He met his untimely death in a war against his own father (2 Samuel 18). What a sad ending, but the danger of self-promotion will always end in a disaster. And what greater example than Lucifer the Archangel?

In the Bible, it is written that the devil's time is short. This phrase is mentioned in the book of Revelation, which describes the end of the world and the ultimate triumph of good over evil. In *Revelation*

12:12, it says "Therefore rejoice, ye heavens, and ye that dwell in them. Woe to the inhabiters of the earth and of the sea! for the devil is come down unto you, having great wrath, because he knoweth that he hath but a short time." This passage suggests that the devil knows he has only a limited time left before his ultimate defeat, and so he is filled with rage and seeks to do as much damage as he can before his time is up.

SHOULD WE SEEK GREAT THINGS FOR OURSELVES, OR SHOULD WE NOT SEEK THEM?

Jeremiah 45:5 says, "And seekest thou great things for thyself? seek them not: for, behold, I will bring evil upon all flesh, saith the Lord: but thy life will I give unto thee for a prey in all places whither thou goest."

Self-promotion is a very common flaw among ministries, politicians, and leaders in general. In this scripture above, God warns a very smart but ambitious scribe not to seek great things for himself, but rather *seek the kingdom of God and His righteousness, and the things will be added (Matthew 6:33).* This verse also reminds us that we should not seek after worldly success and riches, as they can distract us from what is truly important in life. Instead, we should focus on living a life that is pleasing to God and trust in Him to guide and protect us through all circumstances, even in times of hardship and suffering. Ultimately, our true treasure and hope lies in our relationship with God and not in the temporary pleasures of this world.

I have seen the destruction of many who promoted themselves because ministry was never about souls or winning souls; to them, it was all about status and position in the kingdom.

When leaders self-promote without accountability, they are setting themselves up for failure. *To whom much is given, much more is required (Luke 12:48).* Most of the time, when folk self-promote, they desire power. There's very little talk today in many circles about humility; it's the missing component in leadership. Humility is the way to take the low seat and prefer your brother.

Being humble in ministry can be challenging, especially when you are in a leadership position. However, there are a few things that you can do to cultivate humility:

1. **Recognize your humanity:** Remember that you are not perfect, and you make mistakes. Be honest about your limitations and weaknesses.

2. **Value others:** Treat everyone with respect and kindness, no matter their position or status. Be willing to listen to others and learn from them.

3. **Serve others:** Look for opportunities to serve those around you. Put the needs of others before your own.

4. **Give credit to others:** When things go well, give credit to your team. Don't take all the credit for yourself.

5. **Stay connected to God:** Remember that you are serving God, not yourself. Stay connected to Him through prayer, worship, and Bible study.

By focusing on these things, you can cultivate a spirit of humility in your ministry. Remember, humility is not about being weak or timid. It's about recognizing that everything you have is a gift from God and using it to serve others.

I want to encourage this next generation to keep serving, stay faithful, and let God exalt you in due season. *Don't grow weary in your well-being; you will reap if you faint not (Galatians 6:9-10).* Stay under your leader and wait for God to open a door. When God opens a door, no man can shut it (Rev. 3:8). I have known younger preachers leave their spiritual covering and go outside their camp to someone they don't know so that they can get a position without going through the process. In my conclusion, self-promotion equals self-destruction.

CHAPTER XIII

THE ULTIMATE TEST- REAL TEST

BISHOP RON WEBB'S PERSPECTIVE

Nobody enjoys correction, but if we don't listen to the correction God sends, He will start dealing with or correcting us Himself. On the other hand, when correction is taken as a personal attack, it is rendered ineffective. Rather than focusing on the problem, the individual may become defensive or even hostile, making it harder to find a solution. It's important to remember that correction is not meant to be a personal attack, but rather an opportunity to learn and grow. By approaching correction with humility and an open mind, we can become better versions of ourselves and build stronger relationships with those around us.

Hebrews 12:6 says, "For whom the Lord loveth he chasteneth, and scourgeth every son whom he receiveth."

Correction is not hatred; it's an act of love, and that's why there is so much immorality in the church: there is no correction or accountability. Why is it that no one wants correction? The spirit of pride. We like telling but hate being told. It takes humility to receive correction.

Can you be corrected without retaliation? Being able to take correction is a great sign of humility; your leader doesn't just give you direction but also gives you correction.

The real question is how do you respond to correction?
Do you receive it?
Do you feel beaten down?
Do you get defensive?
Do you fall into self-pity?
Let's face it: accepting correction is hard. It's easy to think we know best and no one has the right to tell us to change, and most of the time, we interpret correction as judgment.

Correction and judgment are two different things. Correction is meant to help us grow and learn from our mistakes, while judgment is meant to condemn and punish us for our mistakes. Correction is done with the intention of guiding us toward a better path, while judgment is done with the intention of making us feel guilty or ashamed for our actions. Correction is done out of love and care, while judgment is done out of anger and resentment. It's important to understand the difference between correction and judgment so that we can approach correction with humility and an open heart, rather than feeling attacked or condemned.

1. When we're not open to correction, it can hinder our Christian walk.
2. If we don't acknowledge we made a mistake and change our ways, it can have negative consequences.

Proverbs 15:32 says, "He that refuseth instruction despiseth his own soul: but he that heareth reproof getteth understanding."

In addition, if we don't obey authority figures in our lives, such as our parents, teachers, pastors, etc., it will be very hard to obey God. In fact, God places authority figures in our lives to guide us and to mentor us.

Hebrews 12:11 says that no discipline seems pleasant for or at the time but painful later on. However, it produces a harvest of righteousness and peace for those who have been trained by it.

Always keep an attitude that's open to instruction and correction. Without it, you can never improve and grow. On the other hand, God uses correction to break our spirit of pride. I know it's not easy to receive but it can be the very thing that stops us from moving to the next level.

Learn to accept it even when you don't feel like you need it, humble yourself, and receive it.

Jesus rebuked Peter on several occasions. Jesus rebuked him when he said that he was going to cross. Jesus had just revealed to His disciples for the first time the plan: He was to go to Jerusalem to suffer, die, and be raised to life (Matthew 16:21; Mark 8:31). Peter said, "Oh no." Jesus said, "Get thee behind me, satan." Yet Peter continued following Jesus. Now the question is, can your leader correct you as the Father corrects His son or daughter without you leaving the church, getting upset or offended, whether you're publicly or privately rebuked? If you accept it, things will work out for you in the long run.

REASONS TO EMBRACE CORRECTION

1. It will keep you out of ignorance.
Proverbs 12:1 says, "Whoever loves instruction loves knowledge but he who hates correction is stupid."

Proverbs 15:5 says, "A fool dispises his father's instruction open rebuke is better than secret love."

2. It's good for personal growth and development.
3. Correction can help us learn from our mistakes, improve our skills, and become better versions of ourselves.
4. Help us build stronger relationships with others, as it shows that we value their input and feedback.

2 TYPES OF DISCIPLINE- DISCIPLINE BY OTHERS AND SELF-DISCIPLINE

Discipline by others refers to being held accountable by someone else for your actions. For example, a teacher may discipline a student for misbehaving in class. On the other hand, self-discipline refers to the ability to control your own behavior and stick to a set of rules or principles without external influence. It requires a certain level of self-awareness and willpower to stay on track and avoid distractions or temptations. Both types of discipline can be important for personal and professional development, but self-discipline is often considered more valuable in the long run as it allows individuals to take owner-ship of their actions and achieve their goals independently.

But we must not despise chastening. God had a plan and a purpose. Pruning produces much fruit (John 15:1-8).

Never in your life will it be without correction, and if you're going to operate in ministry, you have to stay open to correction. There have been more church splits and divisions because no one wants to listen.

CHAPTER XIV

HONOR

BISHOP RON WEBB'S PERSPECTIVE

Any nation that forgets God will perish, but *blessed is the nation where God is their Lord (Psalm 33:12)*. Dishonor and disrespectful people only live to themselves and no one else. Honor has been lost and so badly needs to be restored. Our country has been blessed beyond measure. A great part of which has honored God, but now we are watching our land become curse because we are slowly, or shall I say quickly, sinking into a place of dishonor. This is not a path we should tread lightly, for the consequences of dishonor are severe and far-reaching.

We were taught to honor the *hoary, gray head, the head of wisdom (Proverbs 16:31)*. Now, this younger generation does not know or understand the value of honor. Please, young leaders who aspire to become great leaders, do not try to step over or around the older leaders. Honor them for their service, labor, longevity in the ministry, or leadership, and in return, God will honor you. Remember, the rewards of honor are not just spiritual, but they can also manifest in your leadership journey, bringing you success and fulfillment.

Young leaders can honor the older generation by recognizing and respecting their wisdom, experience, and contributions. They can seek out their guidance and mentorship, listen to their stories, and show appreciation for the foundation they have laid. Additionally, young leaders can honor the older generation by acknowledging their achievements and demonstrating humility and a willingness to learn from those who have come before them.

I Samuel 2:30 says, "Therefore the LORD, the God of Israel, declares: 'I promised that your house and the house of your father should go in and out before me forever,' but now the LORD declares: 'Far be it from me, for those who honor me I will honor, and those who despise me shall be lightly esteemed."

The law of sowing and reaping is a biblical principle. It essentially states that whatever a person sows, they will also reap. In other words, the actions and choices a person makes will have corresponding consequences. If someone sows positivity, kindness, and generosity, they can expect to reap similar benefits in return. Conversely, if someone sows negativity, selfishness, and dishonesty, they will likely face negative repercussions. It is a law of sowing and reaping. You get what you sow after you sow. You get what you give out. *Malachi 1:6 says, "A son honors his father, and a slave his master. If I am a father, where is the honor due me? If I am a master, where is the respect due me?" says the Lord Almighty. "It is you priests who show contempt for my name. "But you ask, 'How have we shown contempt for your name?"*

Once you discover the greatness of honor and what its benefits will do for your life, you will embrace it quickly. If there is order in the courts, then let there be honor in the house of God.

The benefits of honor are numerous and significant. When you honor others, you will likely receive respect and appreciation. Honoring someone can also strengthen relationships, build trust, and foster a positive and supportive environment. Additionally, being known as a person who honors others can enhance your reputation and open up opportunities for collaboration and leadership. Practicing honor can lead to a more harmonious and fulfilling personal and professional life.

There has been a tremendous loss of honor and respect for authority. Society dishonors those in authority in various ways. Some common examples include:

Disregarding their experience and wisdom: Society sometimes dismisses the knowledge and expertise of those in authority, especially if they belong to older generations. This can lead to a lack of respect for their insights and contributions.

Undermining their leadership: There can be a tendency to undermine the leadership of those in authority, whether it's in the workplace, community, or government. This can manifest as resistance to their decisions or a lack of support for their initiatives.

Public criticism and ridicule: With the prevalence of social media and public platforms, those in authority often face public criticism, ridicule, and even personal attacks. This can erode the respect and honor that should be afforded to them.

Failure to provide necessary support: In some cases, society fails to provide the necessary support and resources to those in authority, making it challenging for them to carry out their responsibilities effectively.

These actions can contribute to a culture of dishonor and disrespect towards those in authority, ultimately undermining the stability and functionality of various institutions and organizations.

WHAT IS HONOR?

To regard and respect.

To give special recognition.

To value or place a high price on something or someone.

From the Hebrew to Greek – an ornament of splendor or majesty excellency.

Also, it means to be heavy or weighted. People of honor carry weight. Some are heavyweights in the Kingdom of God.

If you give honor, you will receive honor. In the gospel, sons and daughters honor their spiritual parents.

DON'T DISHONOR – CURSE OF DISHONORING

The Bible is filled with people who dishonored God and authority figures.

1. Miriam dishonored Moses and was struck with leprosy (Numbers 12).
2. The captains and their men dishonored Elisha, mocked him, and were consumed by the fire of the Lord (2 King 1).
3. Ananias and Sapphira dishonored the Holy Ghost and Peter. They dropped dead at his feet (Acts 5).
4. Korah and his Klan were swallowed up because they dishonored and disrespected their leaders (Numbers 16).
5. When churches do not take care of their leadership, they dishonor them. Take care of their financial needs.

Philippians 4:16-19 says, "For even when I was in Thessalonica, you sent me aid more than once when I was in need. Not that I desire your gifts; what I desire is that more be credited to your account. I have received full payment and have more than enough. I am amply supplied, now that I have received from Epaphroditus the gifts you sent. They are a fragrant offering, an acceptable sacrifice, pleasing to God. And my God will meet all your needs according to the riches of his glory in Christ Jesus."

Paul knew that if they gave and took care of his needs, God would give back to them by supplying their needs. In *1 Timothy 5:18, it says, "Do not muzzle the ox that treads out the corn."*

CHAPTER XV

THE NEED FOR HEALING – WHAT IS THE REMEDY?

BISHOP ADRIAN RODGERS' PERSPECTIVE

As a Pastor, not only is it my assignment to guide the fatherless, but it is also my responsibility to recognize the tendencies in those who are unaware that the behavior they show is linked to the absence they experienced earlier in life. I must aid them in unpeeling the layers of insecurity, rejection and a host of other behaviors that are a result of a past with deficits. It is easy sometimes to stop others' deficiencies because, all of us, according to Jahari's window, have blind spots. Because they remain hidden to us, it takes the power of God and His word to expose these areas. It also takes discernment and, many times, counseling to bring these places to the surface to begin the healing. Many believe healing is the feeling of the absence of pain. However, as I mature as a person and a pastor, I realize that healing is not always the absence of pain; it is also the MANAGEMENT of pain. Not only have I experienced it personally, which aids in my approach to pastoring and counseling, but I have experienced it vicariously through the lives of those whom I am in a close relationship with. Pain has a way of spreading to others, which we call sympathy. Empathy is when it is not just their experience, in some way or form; you have that same expression of pain.

The need for healing begins with knowing that healing is needed; only a sick person goes to see the doctor. The Bible says in *Matthew 9:12c (The King James Version), "They that be whole need not a physician, but they that are sick."*

Until a person knows they need a Father, they will not search for one. This need lives in the unknown and blind self as aforementioned as a part of Jahori's window. How does a person know they need a Father?

1. They are without a father or a strong male mentor.

2. Failed male relationships, particularly submitting to male authority on the job, in the church, and in the home.

3. They show rebellion when corrected.

4. They are uncommitted to church membership.

5. They will leave or disfellowship if they are corrected or offended.

Bringing a father figure or a male mentor in your life requires a lot of prayer. You need the right father. Your current pastor should be your first consideration; this should have been the person who sent you out to become a pastor. You should not start a church without your Pastor's blessings, knowledge, and support. Starting a church is not a decision that should be taken lightly or without prayer and advice. Just like a son or daughter should not leave their parents' home without their blessings, knowledge, and support. Starting a church right requires the guidance of a spiritual father because it is so much more than just preaching. Some people who are pastoring now are not anointed to pastor but are great preachers who know how to draw a crowd.

As a result, they keep a crowd, but it is always a different crowd. They will have phenomenal services, but after the service, there is no structure, vision, or leadership because the anointing to pastor is not on them. A real spiritual father would know this in the beginning. If there is an anointing to pastor, leadership is still needed. A Pastor needs a Pastor before he starts and as he is walking it out. Several members of my family, including my late wife and I, were riding with my father one day when he said that there needed to be a church in Jonesboro, AR and Southaven, MS. At that time, my Father was already leading two congregations 45 minutes apart, I was serving as Minister of Music for both, Associate Pastor for one, and we were running up and down the highway several days a week.

I am the oldest of my siblings, so I spoke up and said to my father that he could go to Jonesboro, AR, and Southaven, MS. However, we were tired and would not be accompanying him, not knowing that God had a plan. I had no plans to ever pastor. I wanted to play the organ and assist my Father forever as far as I was concerned. A year later, while in Rapid City, SD, my wife, and I were prophesied to concerning pastoring as a team. My father said it was not time yet, so we continued to serve where we were. Two years later on a Thursday night while in a church service, God spoke to me and said you go to Jonesboro now. I called my father the next day and told him what God told me. There was an agreement in his spirit. The following Wednesday my father and I were in Jonesboro, AR looking at the city, visited the Chamber of Commerce, found a facility to hold services, and a station to do a weekly radio broadcast.

God blessed the start of the new ministry because we didn't sneak off and start. Also, we did not try to pull members out of the home church. God does not subtract from churches to start another one. He adds and then multiplies. Of course your family should accompany you, but no one else without your Pastor's approval. Everything fell into place because it was God's timing and because we did it in order with the blessing, knowledge and support of my father and pastor.

Everything in the natural or spiritual is about order. Order is defined as an authoritative direction or instruction, command, or mandate. (dictionary.com)

The Bible says in *Genesis 8:22 (KJV), "²² While the earth remaineth, seedtime and harvest, and cold and heat, and summer and winter, and day and night shall not cease."* In other words, God set the earth up to run in order. He said while the earth remaineth or for as long as the earth exists. You see to wear shorts in the winter or a fur coat in the summer is doing things out of season. With God, it never goes from fall to summer or spring to winter because He is all about order. The Bible also says in *1 Corinthians 14:40 (The King James Version), "⁴⁰ Let all things be done decently and in order."* If God keeps repeating something, it is not because He has run out of words to say. It is because He's trying to drive home a point. The word order is mentioned in the Bible 61 times, so evidently, order is essential to God.

Once you have heard from God, you should go and speak with this person and ask them to pray about being your spiritual father. They must pray for confirmation as well. The father and the son or daughter will need to know this is the right decision because this is an important life choice. Please understand that every son or daughter needs a spiritual father. Bill Riedel, the founding and lead pastor of Redemption Hill Church in Washington, D.C., states that "spiritual fathers discipline their sons" (Riedel, 2019). Within the Bible, the Apostle Paul positioned himself as a father throughout his letters, speaking to his spiritual sons. He consistently provided a corrective influence, while not provoking or embittering people unnecessarily (Riedel, 2019).

According to the article *"Young Pastors Need Spiritual Fathers,"* Apostle Paul was able to provide love and discipline that was free from shame. While providing love and discipline, he also urged course corrections and behavioral changes to those he led. While it is said suggestions may be easily discarded when someone disagrees with them, spiritual fathers should be respected highly. They are also given authority and even sought out for correction (Riedel, 2019).

Having a spiritual father can lovingly and patiently challenge someone and allow for penetrating questions to be asked in order to expose deeper heart issues within life and ministry, and calls for a greater repentance, discipline, and integrity (Riedel, 2019). Not having a spiritual father who can discipline and speak life, creates a dangerous place to be in.

Over the years I have gone back to my father several times for advice. Getting advice does not make me feel less than a man. The Bible says in *Proverbs 11:14 (KJV), "Where no counsel is, the people fall: but in the multitude of counselors there is safety."* Once a mentor or spiritual covering has been established, it does not mean that further advice is not needed. There is no graduation from spiritual covering. It is unwise to only hear yourself when pondering important life matters. For instance, concerning my personal life, marriage, child rearing, major financial decisions and pastoral matters, my father has and remains a source of stability and wisdom.

There were times in my marriage that I solicited advice and prayers from my father because he has proven to be trustworthy and full of wisdom. My father had been married to my biological mother for more than seven years before she passed away. He remarried an amazing woman who finished raising my siblings and me. They have been married for over 52 years. Before my wife, Susan Woods-Rodgers passed, we were married for over 33 years. Please note that at the time of this release I was blessed to marry a beautiful woman, Constance DeBerry-Rodgers, in November of 2020. However so, it stands to reason that he would be a reliable source of information.

Many years ago, I was falsely accused of having a child outside of wedlock just before I was married. I received a notice of a certified letter for me at the post office. To my surprise, I was being sued for paternity! I probably read the letter ten times before I called my father. He asked me if I was guilty and I said, "No sir." He then said, "Son you must immediately speak with your wife." He instructed me not to run from this, but to be upfront and honest. Honestly, I felt sorry for her, but I knew I was not her father. I went to the church office, handed my wife the letter and we talked about it. She asked me if it was true and I answered, "No." This situation had the potential to be embarrassing and cause a rift in my family. However, I had the encouragement and support of my father and wife. After taking a DNA test, I was totally exonerated. At the time of the allegations, the child was 16 years old and still did not know who her father was.

My parents raised four children. So, since my late wife and I had young children at the time, we sought the advice of the parents who raised us. My mother-in-law raised ten children almost by herself, so we certainly sought advice from her as well. So many times, people who have not been raised with a father are taught that they do not need anyone to assist them. This thought process leads to multiple mistakes and bad experiences. There is an old saying that says, "Experience is not the best teacher, but fools learn by no other way; everyone should refuse to play the role of a fool."

My father is an excellent businessman. We were raised in a comfortable home and lived an upper middle-class life. Nothing was ever repossessed or disconnected. As a newly married 20-year-old, I needed a lot of financial advice. I grew tired of my finances being up and down as a result of making foolish decisions, so I sought the advice of someone who was doing it well.

Bishop Charles Rodgers, my father, has been my pastor since he started when I was four years old. He successfully pastored for almost 50 years. Why would he not be one of those that I went to when I felt like I was in over my head or before I made a major decision? I remember once I had a board member who was being a serious problem and I decided he needed to be removed from the board. I called my father and discussed with him what the board member had done. He asked one question, "Do you have proof?" I answered, "No, but I know he did it." My father then instructed me that I could not proceed to remove the board member without absolute proof. That advice saved me from making a big mistake and ruining what is now a good relationship. Seeking his advice in pastoral matters did not make me less of a pastor. It made me a better-informed pastor. My father and pastor is not the only person that I get advice from, but he is certainly at the top of the list.

A spiritual father not only provides discipline but according to Bill Riedel they breathe courage into their sons. For example, Timothy was reminded by Paul to *"fan into flame the gift of God, which is in you through the laying on of my hands" (2 Tim. 1:6)*. Spiritual fathers breathe courage into their struggling sons.

According to the article, Bill Kynes was a source of much encouragement, regularly challenging those around him to leave fear and shame behind and to embrace the power of God's Spirit to move toward love, self-control, and a willingness to share in Christ's sufferings.

The article also supports the importance of spiritual guidance and communicates that church planters and young pastors are missing out if they don't seek out and submit to more seasoned spiritual fathers. It is also encouraged for older and wiser pastors to invest in the younger generation and younger men who can grow up under them in ministry. Those who are older and seasoned need to be on the front line saying, *"Imitate me as I imitate Christ" (1 Cor. 11:1) (Riedel, 2019).*

The article then went on to express that Bill needed an older mentor and the accountability of sitting under the authority of godly elders as he set out to plant a church. However, to Bill's surprise, God gave him more than he hoped for with the gift of a spiritual father further proving the point that young church planters should seek out the blessing of spiritual fathers for themselves (Riedel, 2019).

CONCLUSION

Some Pastors, like many children in our world today, are illegitimate. This move has created chaos in the kingdom. It is imperative that those who are pastoring be spiritually fathered. Again, the question remains how can you father if you have not been fathered? Unfortunately, the spirit of a bastard is to run from correction, teaching, and sometimes even encouragement. That's why it remains vital to submit to a spiritual father and be covered not for your good but also for the good of those that you influence.

As pastors and leaders in ministry, we often find ourselves in positions of authority and influence. It can be easy to become defensive or resistant when faced with criticism or correction. However, embracing growth and learning from feedback is essential for personal and spiritual development. Correction, when received with humility and openness, can lead to transformation and maturity in our ministries.

When we shift our perspective and view correction as a gift rather than a burden, we open ourselves up to a world of growth and possibility. Correction is not an indication of failure but an opportunity for refinement and improvement. It allows us to uncover blind spots, sharpen our skills, and deepen our faith. Embracing correction in ministry is a courageous act that shows our commitment to continuous growth and excellence. By welcoming feedback with open hearts and minds, we create an environment where transformation can flourish, leading to stronger relationships, impactful ministry, and a brighter future ahead.

When we choose to view correction as a valuable tool for our personal and spiritual growth, we unlock the potential for transformation and refinement in our ministry. Each correction and feedback received is an opportunity for us to cultivate humility, resilience, and a deeper reliance on God's grace. Embracing correction in this light allows us to not only improve our ministry skills but also strengthen our character and faith. It shapes us into more effective and compassionate leaders, guiding us towards a path of continuous learning and development. Building a community where feedback is welcomed and embraced can lead to greater unity, trust, and effectiveness in our shared mission. Fathers are important and every pastor needs a leader they can submit to. In closing, don't pastor if you value the dynamics of a healthy father-child relationship, having accountability, and humility.

ABOUT THE AUTHOR

Adrian R. Rodgers was born and raised in Memphis, TN. He is the son of Bishop and Mrs. Charles Rodgers and the grandson of three pastors. He began his ministry as a musician. He started playing the drums for his father's church at the age of 5. He moved from the drums to the piano and finally to the organ. He served as Minister of Music at his father's church for 15 years.

Adrian's life took a divine turn when God shifted his focus from music to the preaching ministry. He served as an Associate Pastor for Bishop Rodgers for eight years, during which he began to evangelize as God started to shape his deliverance ministry. In 1992, the Spirit of God spoke to Bishop Charles Rodgers about planting a ministry in Jonesboro, AR. In 1994, the Spirit of God spoke directly to Adrian, calling him to begin the work in Jonesboro, AR. He obediently started with a daily broadcast in May of the same year. In September, he and his then-wife, Susan, founded Fullness of Joy Ministries, a testament to his unwavering faith and commitment.

In January 2008, Pastor Adrian Rodgers's call to ministry became greater. His father, Bishop Rodgers, retired from full-time pastorate, and Pastor Rodgers became the pastor of New Dimensions Ministries in Memphis, TN. Ten years ago, he was consecrated to the office of Bishop and became the Presiding Bishop of Impact Fellowship.

His academic achievements further exemplify Adrian's commitment to his ministry. He is a proud graduate of the International College of Bible Theology, holding an Associates degree. His thirst for knowledge led him to pursue and successfully obtain Bachelor's, Master's, and Doctorate degrees from Adullam Bible College. His dedication to spreading the word of God extends beyond borders, as he is a popular conference speaker and foreign evangelist. He has been a part of several mission trips bi-annually to Manila, Philippines and Africa, Costa Rica, Belize, Central America and Columbia, South America, a testament to his global impact.

Adrian and Susan were married for over 33 years, and from their union, two children were born: Adrian Charles and Brianna Danielle. Later on, their daughter-in-law Lisa joined the family. After Susan went to be with the Lord after being alone for a while, Adrian asked, and God showed him his next partner in Life and Ministry, Constance Dixon DeBerry, and they have been married since November 2020. From this union, Adrian has four bonus children: Julius, Jonathan, Jennifer, and Jasmine; one son-in-law, Clinton; two daughters-in-law, Jessica and Jai; and now ten grandchildren.

ABOUT THE AUTHOR

Dr. Ron Webb is the pastor of the Mt. Calvary Powerhouse Church in Poplar Bluff, Missouri. Pastor Webb has been in the ministry for over 35 years. The unique ministry of Dr. Ron Webb is evident as he is anointed in the area's leadership and church government. Dr. Webb has been considered by many to be A Pastor to Pastors. His ministry is centered around Restoration and Racial Reconciliation and a sincere belief that we must Reach the Lost at Any Cost. His preaching and teaching focuses on empowerment and hope. He often says that church is where you go, but ministry is what you do outside the walls of the church. He believes that with God all things are possible! Dr. Webb has always had a heart for the lost Give me the heathen for my inheritance. Many outreach ministries have been birthed to address the unmet needs of the church and local community. Dr. Webb is an accomplished writer who has authored several books on leadership and racial reconciliation. He is a sought-after speaker, who has ministered the gospel of Christ both national and internationally, including Canada, Haiti, Russia, Jamaica, and England. Dr. Webb is active in the community and has served on both local and state level boards. Dr. Webb is married to Georgia Webb and they have 3 children: Ronnie Webb Jr., Tony Webb and Jackie (Webb) Brown all of Poplar Bluff, Missouri, and 4 grandchildren: Jerrell Brown, Jr.,

Jaxson Brown, Tony Webb and Maleah Webb. In his leisure time, Dr. Webb enjoys fishing and playing sports.

REFERENCES

(n.d.). Retrieved from dictionary.com: https://www.dictionary.com

2020 Merriam-Webster, Incorporated. (n.d.).

Aust, J. (2014, January 8). The Ultimate Purpose of the Family. Retrieved from Beyond Today: https://www.ucg.org/the-good-news/ the-ultimate-purpose-of-the-family

Clegg, R. (2012, October 4). The Corner. Retrieved from National Review.com.

Ditta M. Oliker, P. (2011, June 23). The Importance of Fathers. Retrieved from Psychology Today: https://www. psychologytoday.com/us/blog/the-long-reach-childhood/201106/ the-importance-fathers

Fackerell, M. (2004). Breaking The Bastard Curse. Retrieved from Christian Faith: https://www.christian-faith.com/ breaking-bastard-curse-chapter-9/

Gaille, B. (2017, May 25). 29 Enticing Illegitimate Children Statistics. Retrieved from Brandon Gaille Small

Bussiness and Marketing Advice: https://brandongaille.
com/27-enticing-illegitimate-children-statistics/

Gritters, R. B. (1998, April 26). Loveland Protestant Reformed
Church. Retrieved from The Family:Foundations are Shaking:
https://www.prca.org/articles/family/family_1.html

Nelson, S. (2013, May 6). Census Bureau Links Poverty With
Out-of-Wedlock Births. Retrieved from US News: https://
www.usnews.com/news/newsgram/articles/2013/05/06/
census-bureau-links-poverty-with-out-of-wedlock-births

No, All Those Strollers Aren't Your Imagination. More Women
Are Having Children. (n.d.). Retrieved from Time: https://time.
com/5107704/more-women-mothers/

Peterson, E. H. (2002). The Message Bible. Navpress.

Riedel, B. (2019, DECEMBER 17). Young Pastors Need Spiritual
Fathers. Retrieved from The Gospel Coalition: https://www.
thegospelcoalition.org/article/young-pastors-spiritual-fathers/

Rudnick, A. (2014, 11 20). Why Pastors Need Pastors. Retrieved
from Alan Rudnick: http://www.alanrudnick.org/2014/11/20/
pastors-need-pastors

The King James Version. (n.d.).

The Significance Of A Father's Influence. (2011). Retrieved
from Focus On The Family: https://www.focusonthefamily.com/
family-qa/the-significance-of-a-fathers-influence/

Why Men Matter- Both Now and Forever. (n.d.). Retrieved from
Washington Area Coalition Of Men's Ministries: http://www.
wacmm.org/

Woofenden, L. (2017, 06 30). What Can We Learn From The Story Of Elijah and Elisha. Retrieved from Spiritual Insight For Everyday Life: https://leewoof.org/2017/06/30/what-can-we-learn-from-the-story-of-elijah-and-elisha/

INDEX

www.ingramcontent.com/pod-product-compliance
Lightning Source LLC
Chambersburg PA
CBHW071026120626
46546CB00003B/1231